FLY GUY PRESENTS:
MONSTER TRUCKS

Tedd Arnold

Scholastic Inc.

Just for you, Caedon!

D0057435

Thank you to the following for their contributions to this book: Matthew Gilbert; Dan Allen, Jeff Bialosky, Bill Easterly, John Igras, Jenna Luckey, Chris Mercaldo, Angela Moore, Nicole Pope, Tim Rees, Keith Speller, and Nell Whiting, Feld Motor Sports, Inc.

All photos Monster Jam trucks, equipment, and events © Feld Motor Sports, Inc. All rights reserved. Additional stock photos ©: Dreamstime: 30–31 map (Adrian Brasov), 13 horses (Maria Itina), 13 blue truck (Nerthuz); Shutterstock: 9 tire tracks, and throughout (My Portfolio), 18 burnt paper (Vectorism).

Library of Congress Cataloging-in-Publication Data available

ISBN 978-1-338-35389-1

10 9 8 7 6 5 4 3 2 1   19 20 21 22 23

Printed in the U.S.A.   40
First printing, October 2019

Book design by Sunny Lee and Angela Jun

A boy had a pet fly named Fly Guy.
Fly Guy could say the boy's name —

Buzz and Fly Guy arrived at a big stadium!

"Are you ready to see some monsters?" Buzz asked.

MONSTERZZZZ?!

Fly Guy hid behind Buzz's cap.

"Not those kind of monsters," Buzz explained, giggling. "I'm talking about monster *trucks*."

They raced inside to learn more.

Monster trucks are monster-sized vehicles (VEE-hih-culls) with giant tires. Each monster truck stands nearly 11 feet tall and weighs more than 12,000 pounds.

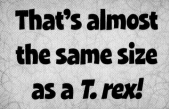

The first monster trucks were built using huge tires called flotation (floh-TAY-shuhn) tires. These tires were originally made to keep big farm equipment from getting stuck in the mud. Today, monster trucks use special versions of these tires made just for competition.

A monster truck tire is 66 inches tall!

WOWZIE!

Having tall tires means monster trucks can climb and roll over just about anything!

Monster trucks can steer with both their front wheels and their back wheels! Each driver uses a steering wheel to control the front wheels. They use switches to control the back wheels.

rear steer switch

Because they have rear steering, monster trucks can make sharp turns and do high-speed spins. These spins are called donuts!

DONUTZ!

A normal car's engine (EHN-jin) is in front, under the hood—but not for most monster trucks! You can usually find a monster truck engine in the middle, behind the driver. This helps keep the truck balanced.

Before the car was invented, people depended on horses to get around. This is where the term "horsepower" comes from. Car companies use horsepower to measure how powerful an engine is. Normal trucks only need the power of 300 horses. A monster truck has five times the horsepower of a normal truck!

X 300

X 300

300 x 5 = 1,500! A monster truck has the power of 1,500 horses!

Monster trucks do a lot of crushing and crashing. Their bodies are usually made of a special type of plastic called fiberglass (FYE-burr-glass). This helps make the trucks lighter and safer.

Custom fiberglass molds can make trucks look like animals or other creatures.

The monster truck Megalodon® has a shark-like body made out of foam!

To be even safer, drivers also wear helmets and fireproof suits!

Monster trucks don't just crush a lot, they cost a lot! The most expensive monster trucks in the world cost almost $300,000 to build.

Making a monster truck also takes time. It can take anywhere from three months to a year to build a monster truck. That's because monster trucks have a lot of different components (cumm-POH-nehnts).

FRAME
The skeleton of the truck!

BODY
Covers the frame of the truck!

CAGE
Protects the driver inside the frame!

ENGINE
Powers the truck!

TIRES
Make the truck roll!

When monster trucks hit the track, they perform all sorts of monster *tricks*. Sometimes it takes years for drivers to master stunts and moves like . . .

"Big Air":
This is when a truck flies through the air, soaring over cars or other obstacles.

The "Wheelie":
This is when a truck drives around on its back wheels.

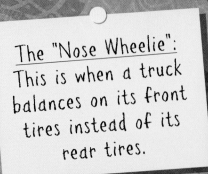

The "Nose Wheelie":
This is when a truck balances on its front tires instead of its rear tires.

The "Backflip":
This is when a truck does a complete flip after speeding up a ramp and then lands safely back on its tires.

The "Bicycle":
This is when a truck balances on two of its side wheels.

Today, monster trucks are pushing the limits with backflips, corkscrews, and two-wheeled tricks.

In 2009, Tom Meents and the truck Maximum Destruction® (Max-D™!), landed the first-ever complete monster truck backflip!

Flipping a 12,000-pound truck is like flipping an elephant!

In 2017, 20-year-old driver Tyler Menninga set the record for the world's longest nose wheelie— over one minute—in the legendary monster truck Grave Digger®!

Performing all those extreme stunts is dangerous. That's why safety is important. Every monster truck has special devices that can turn off its engine in case of an emergency (ee-MUHR-jen-see).

These are called RII's—
Remote Ignition (igg-nish-un)
Interrupters.

RII

A track
official
has a
handheld
RII that
works a
lot like a
cell phone.

OFFICIAL

United States
HOT ROD
Association

BUTTONZZZ!

Monster trucks are not allowed on regular roads because of their size. The tracks inside monster truck arenas and stadiums are custom-made!

Monster trucks race on a J-shaped track, a circle track, or a straight-line track. First to the finish line wins!

○ CIRCLE TRACK ○

○ J-SHAPED TRACK ○

○ STRAIGHT-LINE TRACK ○

Monster truck tires roll best on dirt. Dump trucks deliver it before each event, and front loaders push it around to form hills and ramps.

Track crews use about 15 million pounds of dirt in total!

Once the dirt is set, work trucks come in to lightly water it before the main event. This helps the monster trucks grip the track and pick up speed!

Monster trucks use special gas called methanol (meth-uh-nawl), a fuel made from natural gas. Monster trucks burn two and a half gallons of methanol in under two minutes.

GAZZZ IT UP!

fuel tank

FUEL

FUEL

In "freestyle" events, drivers do as many tricks and stunts as they can before time runs out. These could include jumps, flips, crushing cars, or everyone's favorite: amazing saves! A save is when a driver avoids a crash at the last second.

crushing

save

People all over the world love monster trucks!

In 2002, Paris, France, hosted the first monster truck event outside North America. Since then, monster trucks have toured the globe. There have been races in places like Mexico, Australia, and Japan!

MEXICO

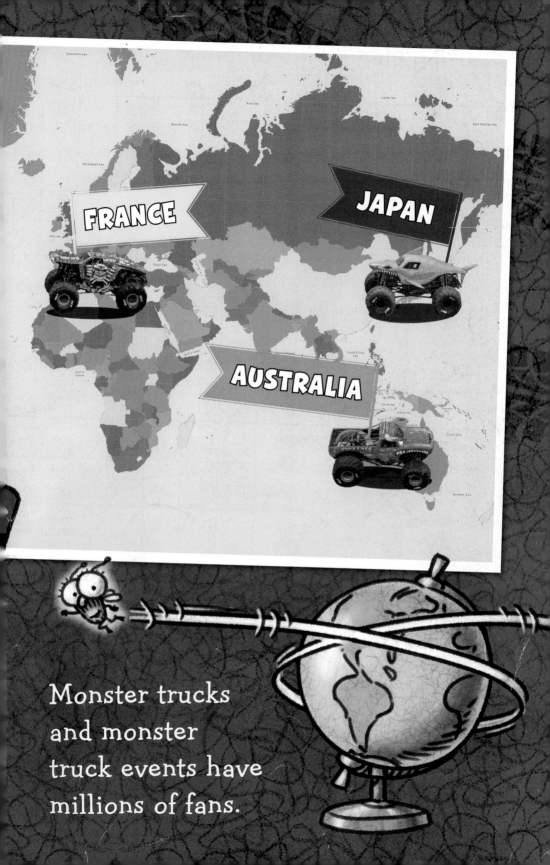

FRANCE

JAPAN

AUSTRALIA

Monster trucks
and monster
truck events have
millions of fans.

"What a wild ride!" said Buzz. "We learned a lot about monster trucks today."

Fly Guy and Buzz could not wait for their next field trip!